ALL ABOARD THE
SOUNDS
TRAIN

Illustrated by
sean sims

cheep cheep

ding dong

Can you find all the birds?

OXFORD
UNIVERSITY PRESS

We're at the station. We're off to explore the different **sounds** all around us.

cheep cheep

ding dong

10/6/23

BRENT LIBRARIES

Please return/renew this item
by the last date shown.
Books may also be renewed by
phone or online.
Tel: 0333 370 4700
ine www.brent.gov.uk/libraryservice

The birds are singing and the cows are grazing in the meadow.

There are sounds all around us.
The rain pitter patters on the windows,
the thunder rumbles and the lightning cracks!

Hurray, now the rain has stopped, we can put on our wellies and play in the puddles. Splish, splash, splosh!

We've arrived at the beach to enjoy the summer sunshine. Let's build sandcastles and play in the sea!

We are so hot in the sun!
It's time to cool down and enjoy our ice-creams.
What sounds do we make?

Now we've arrived in the woods. The wind blows and the autumn leaves rustle and fall.

We're hungry—it's time for tea!
We make noises as we eat, too.
Slurp! Munch! Nibble! Crunch!

We've come to a winter wonderland.
It's so much fun to play in the snow.
We've built a snowman!

It's the end of our journey. We're tired and sleepy.
Everything is quiet and still.

OXFORD

UNIVERSITY PRESS

Great Clarendon Street, Oxford OX2 6DP

Oxford University Press is a department of the University of Oxford.
It furthers the University's objective of excellence in research, scholarship,
and education by publishing worldwide. Oxford is a registered trade mark
of Oxford University Press in the UK and in certain other countries

British Library Cataloguing in Publication Data

Data available

ISBN: 978-0-19-277753-9

1 3 5 7 9 10 8 6 4 2

Printed in China

Paper used in the production of this book is a natural,
recyclable product made from wood grown in sustainable forests.
The manufacturing process conforms to the environmental
regulations of the country of origin.